The Little Manual of Expression with Foam Rubber

Piero Gilardi

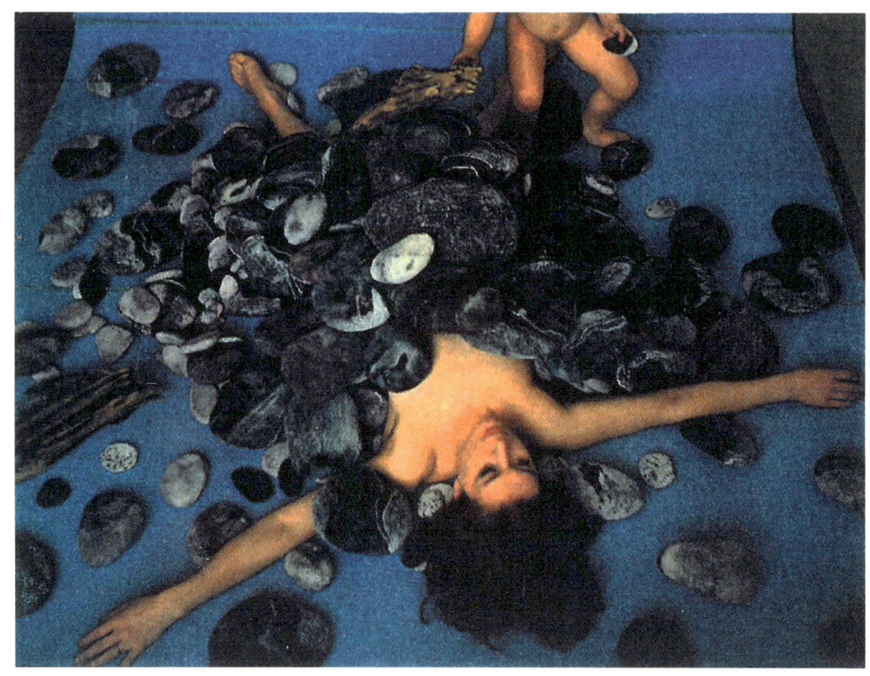

Piero Gilardi, "Vestito di sassi," 1966, performance

WHAT IS FOAM RUBBER?

The most salient characteristics of foam rubber are its elasticity, softness, and lightness. It absorbs shocks and returns to its original shape even if it is repeatedly subjected to traction and torsion. One cubic meter of the least dense foam rubber weighs just 15 kilograms. It appears to us as a warm, ethereal, living material, with dynamic reactions that are to some extent similar to the movements of living organisms.

A synthetic form of flexible foam rubber technically referred to as "expanded polyurethane foam." It is made in large blocks and is the result of a chemical reaction brought about by mixing three liquid components: polyols (petroleum derivatives), diisocyanates, and a foaming agent, which is what gives it its empty-cell structure.

Foam rubber can be bought in shops that sell plastic materials, or from factories specialized in processing the material, and which will cut it to the desired shape and size. The largest blocks of foam rubber can measure up to about 2 x 2 x 1 meters. It can be cut into sheets measuring 2 x 2 meters, as thin as 3 millimeters. When buying foam rubber, one needs to choose not just the right shape and size, but also the density. There are about 10 different densities, ranging from 15 to 50 kilograms per cubic meter.

The choice of density depends on the type of work one intends to do. For example:

T 18 density foam rubber, which is very light but easy to tear, can be used for large sculptures and masks that do not have particular durability requirements and that will not be subjected to considerable physical stress. It is normally white and thus suitable for bright colors, since the pigments used are transparent rather than opaque (rather like watercolor on paper, which makes use of the white background).

T 21 density foam rubber is more robust than T 18 and can be used for making masks, costumes, and puppets, as well as boxed structures. These are made by connecting sheets of the material to form tubes, cylinders, hemispheres, etc. Also this type of foam rubber is generally white.

T 21 E density foam rubber has the same compactness as the previous one, but is more elastic (as indicated by the "E"). This can be used for making masks, puppets, and costumes that will be subjected to torsion and traction, but not for boxed structures, because it has a lower load-bearing strength. It is normally pale yellow in color.

T 21 EE density foam rubber is even more elastic. It is hard to cut and shape with precision because it is so soft, but it can be used to create particularly undulating, mobile shapes. Normally pale orange in color.

T 25 density foam rubber is very compact, with good load-bearing properties. In addition to sculptures with precise carvings and surface treatments, it is also ideal for making boxed structures and large objects that can also be used as seats. It is generally gray, which means that the use of bright, pale colors is limited. Here too it can be found in "E" and "EE"-type densities.

T 50 density foam rubber is extremely compact and long-lasting, so it can be used to make sculpted objects with very precise details and finishes. Since it has good load-bearing qualities, it can be used for those parts of large structures that are most subject to stress. It is normally white.

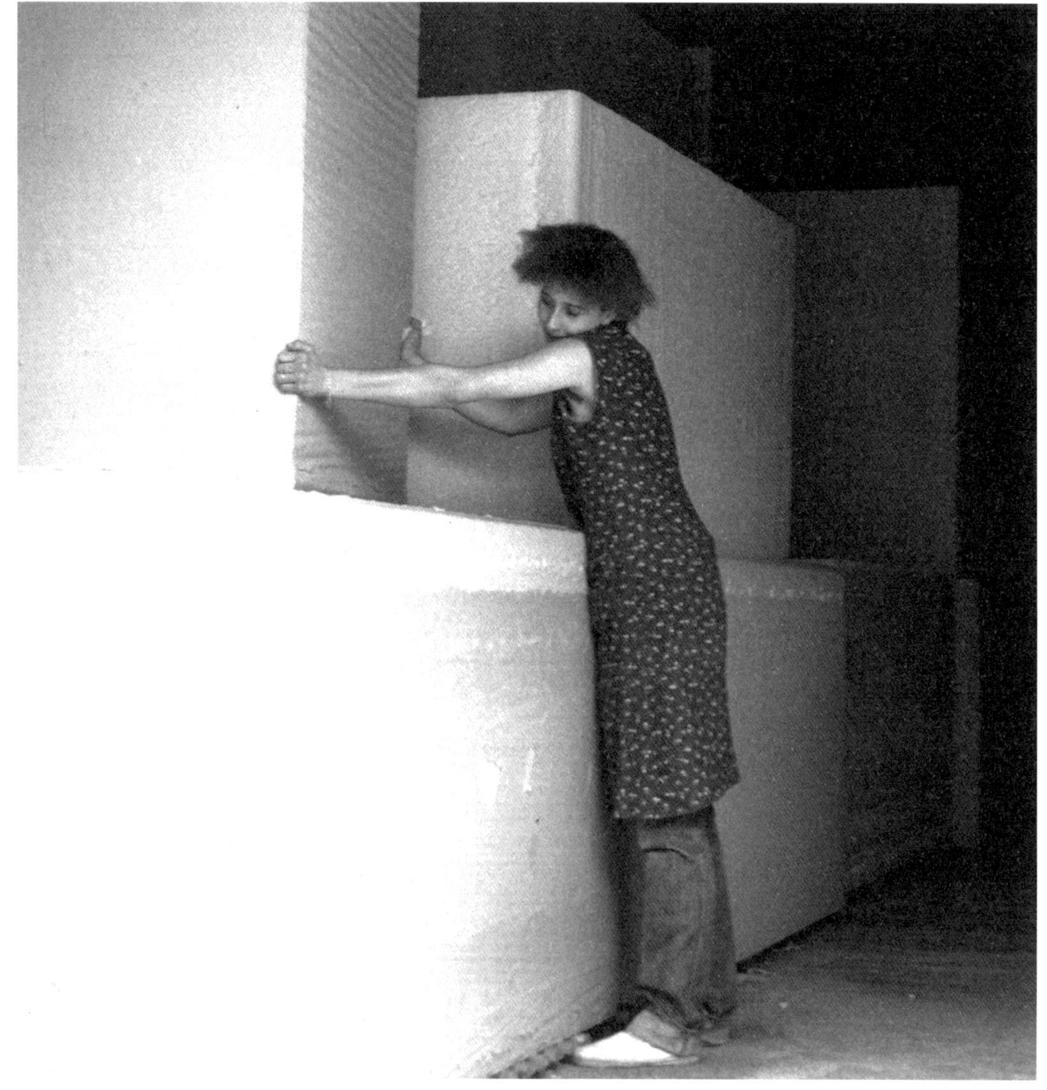

Different densities can of course be used for the same structure, both for construction purposes, to create more solid bases, and to obtain more complex effects of movement, for example by making appendices with more elastic materials.

It is also possible to buy perforated foam rubber with a material structure that is similar to that of sea sponges. Here the colors are more lively: chrome yellow, sky blue, intense pink, orange, and light green. A similar material, known as "moltoprene," can also been bought in sheets. It has a textured surface with bumps or pedicles, with the sheets measuring about 1 x 2 meters and thicknesses varying between 3 and 5 centimeters. They can be used to cover the surfaces of objects both indoors and out, and to cover floors and walls.

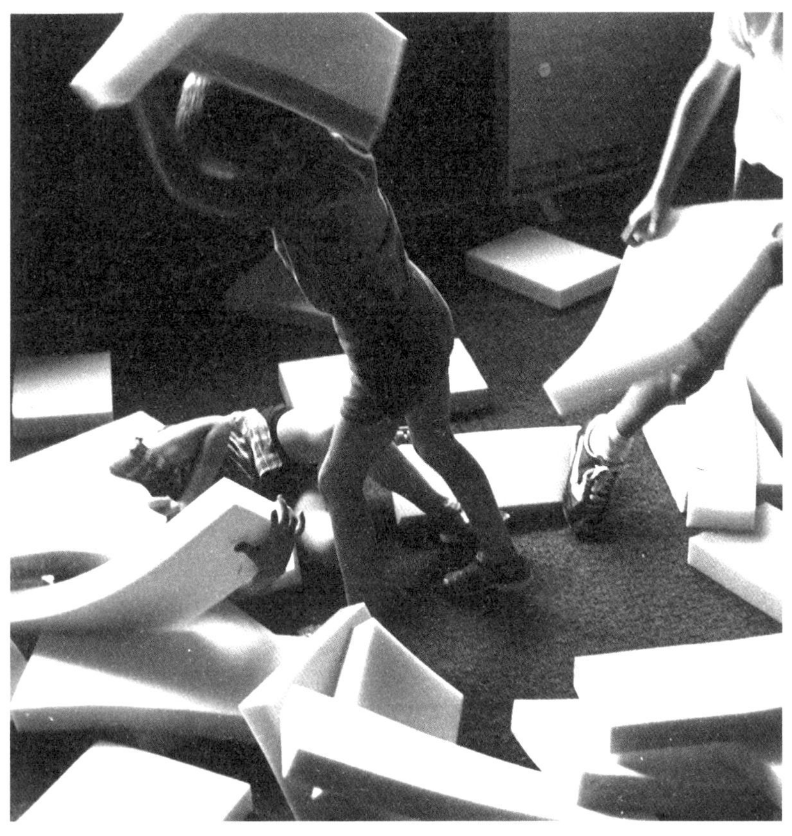

PLAYING WITH FOAM RUBBER

Foam rubber is itself an invitation to play, and a magical, invented material, with sea sponges as its only parallel in our experience of organic nature. It is quite unique and an exception to our general idea of materials created by our culture. Particularly in children, foam rubber evokes a whole series of pleasantly allusive sensations, for example by recalling the softness of the maternal breast. In a sense, pressing it and then letting it reform recalls the childhood idea of "now you see it, now you don't." It can be used as a blunt instrument to give vent to aggression in an innocuous, trouble-free manner.

Playing with scraps or amorphous pieces of foam rubber can help children fully develop their fantasies. A piece of foam rubber might be a safe island in the middle of a menacing "sea" floor or, in another context, it might be a massive boulder to be hurled at the "enemy," or possibly an animal to hug or ride or beat, and so on.

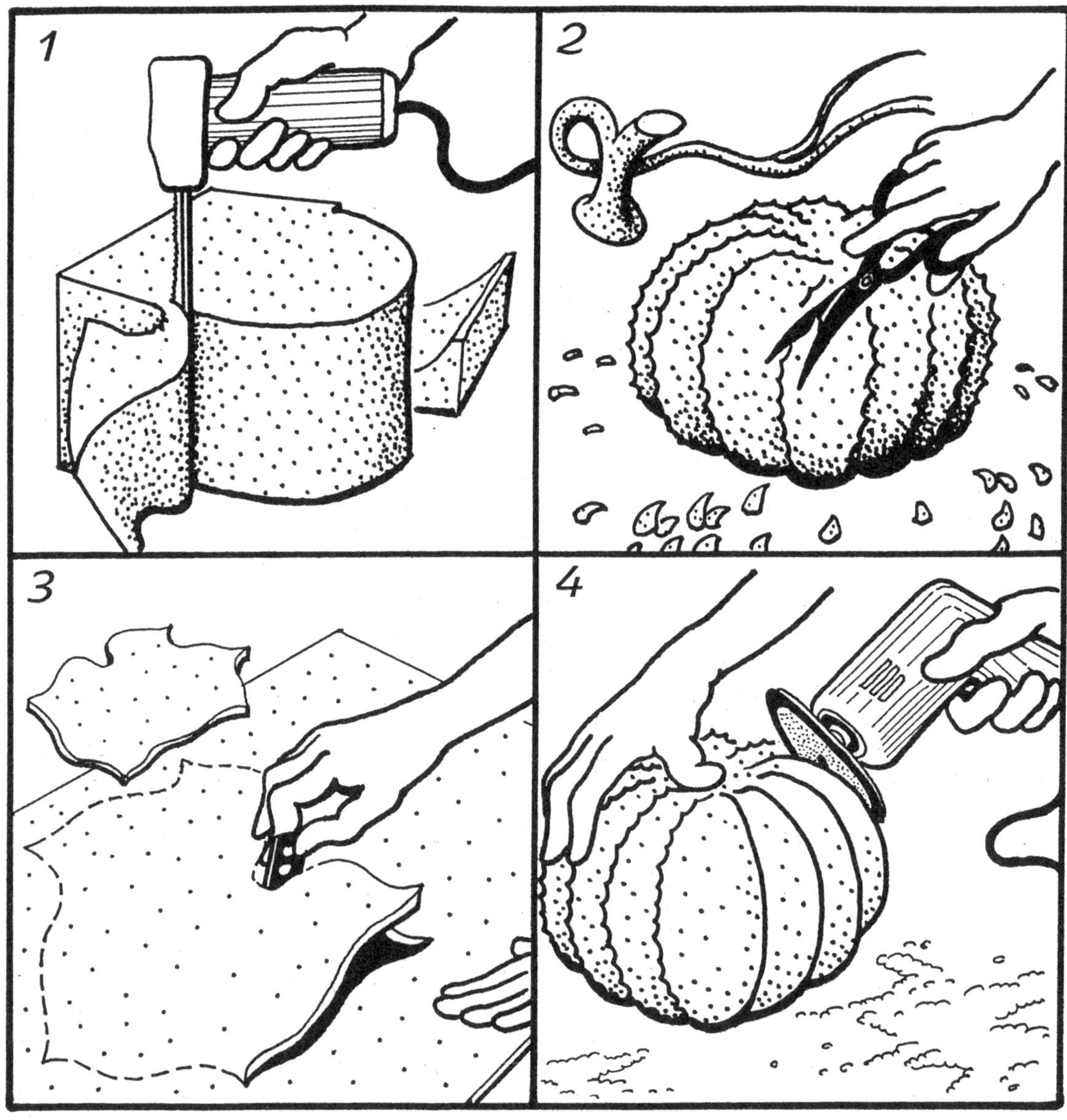

A basic way of working foam rubber is shown in the sequence of drawings from 1 to 8. Start by drawing the outline of the shape you want on a block cut to the approximate size of the object you intend to create. This outline is obtained by working out the orthogonal projections (top view, front view, side view). Then rough out the shape, following the drawn lines, using a special foam-rubber knife or an electric knife with a serrated blade with alternating movement, like that used in the home.

Cut into and remove the foam using round-tipped scissors, which make it easier to create rounded surfaces and, lastly, smooth the foam with a large-grain rotating emery disk applying very little pressure. Thin parts can be obtained by using sheets of foam rubber already cut to the required thickness, cutting them out with a rigid blade or with scissors.

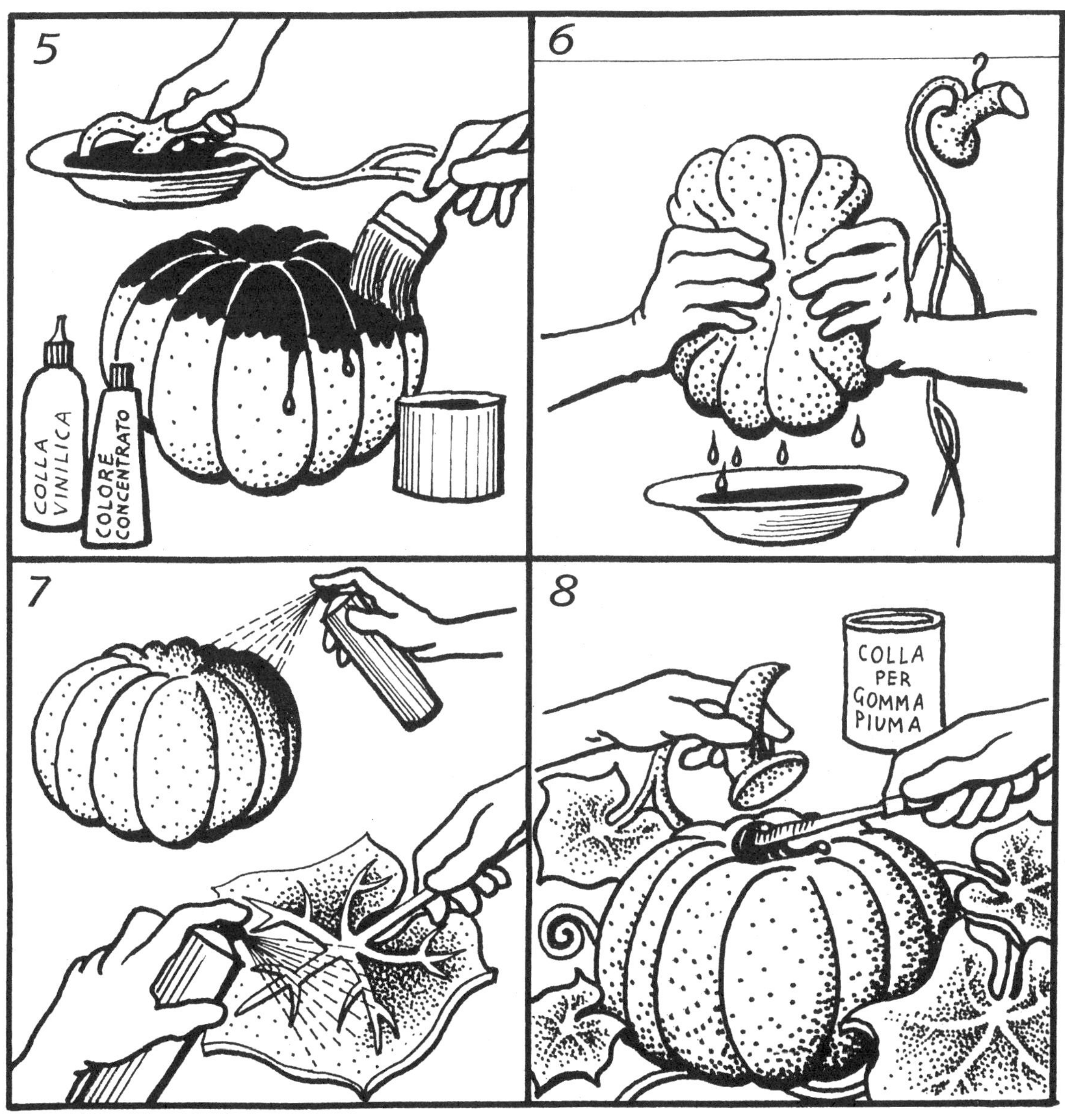

To color foam rubber, made a solution of water (70%), synthetic latex rubber or vinyl resin (30%), and concentrated color for watercolors in the quantity needed to obtain the desired intensity of color. Apply the color in abundant brushstrokes or, better still, by immersing the object in the color. Then turn it round every way to let the color spread out uniformly, or squeeze it like a sponge if you have immersed it in the color. You can also spray on tempera-based color to obtain a rapid result or to perfect the finish. When using this method, you can of course apply cut-out cardboard masks to create details or modular decorations.

The various parts should be assembled only when the color is complete and fully dry, using special foam-rubber glue.

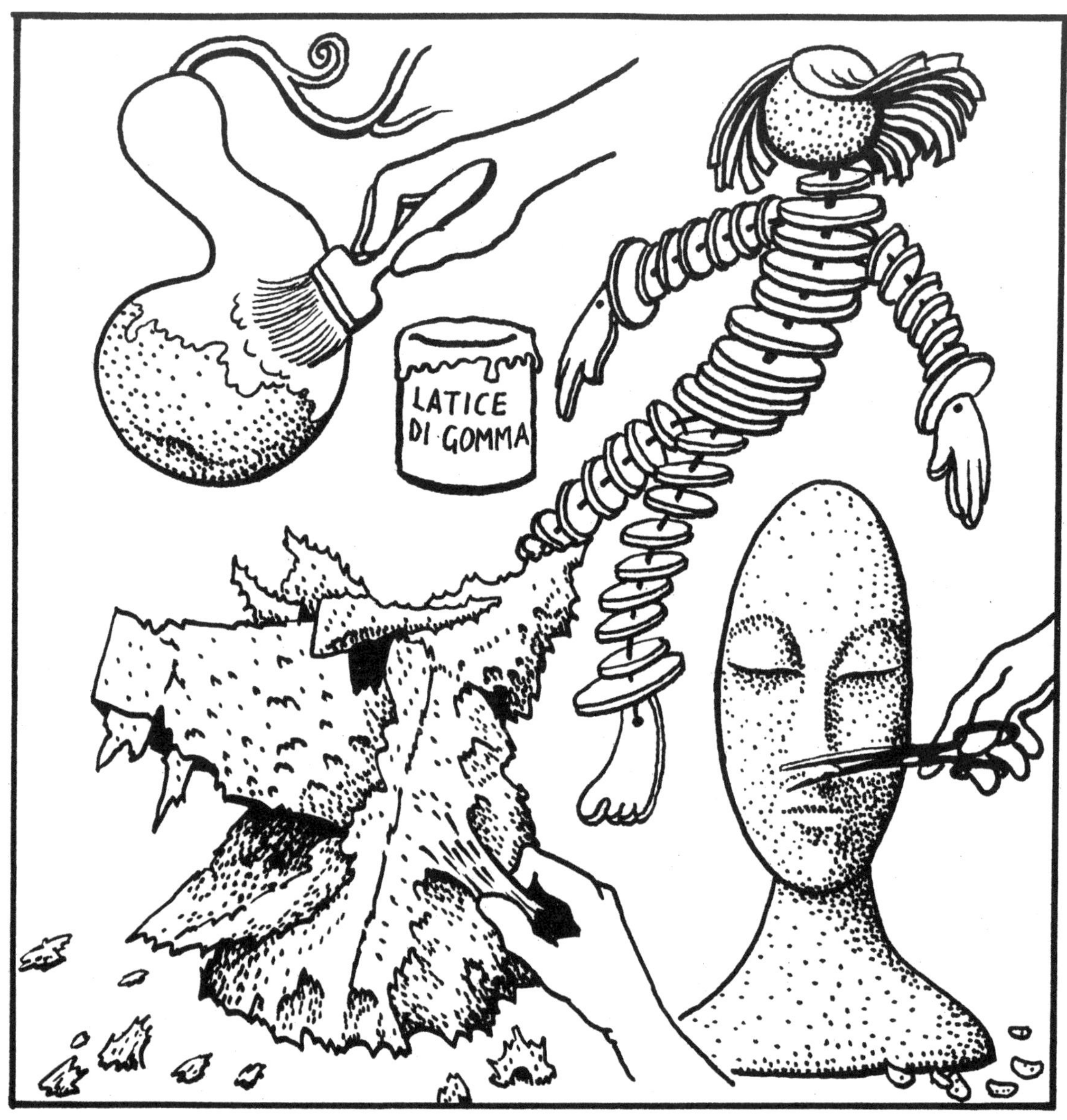

In terms of its potential for expression, the most important features of foam rubber are its softness, flexibility, and lightness. Even though the manipulability of foam-rubber objects clearly offers huge potential, it should be pointed out that the ratio between volume and weight can also be used to create exciting effects of perceptive ambiguity.

Images carved out of foam rubber normally appear as expanded, slightly blurred forms, ephemeral and yet persistent, rather like the contradictory images of the world of dreams.

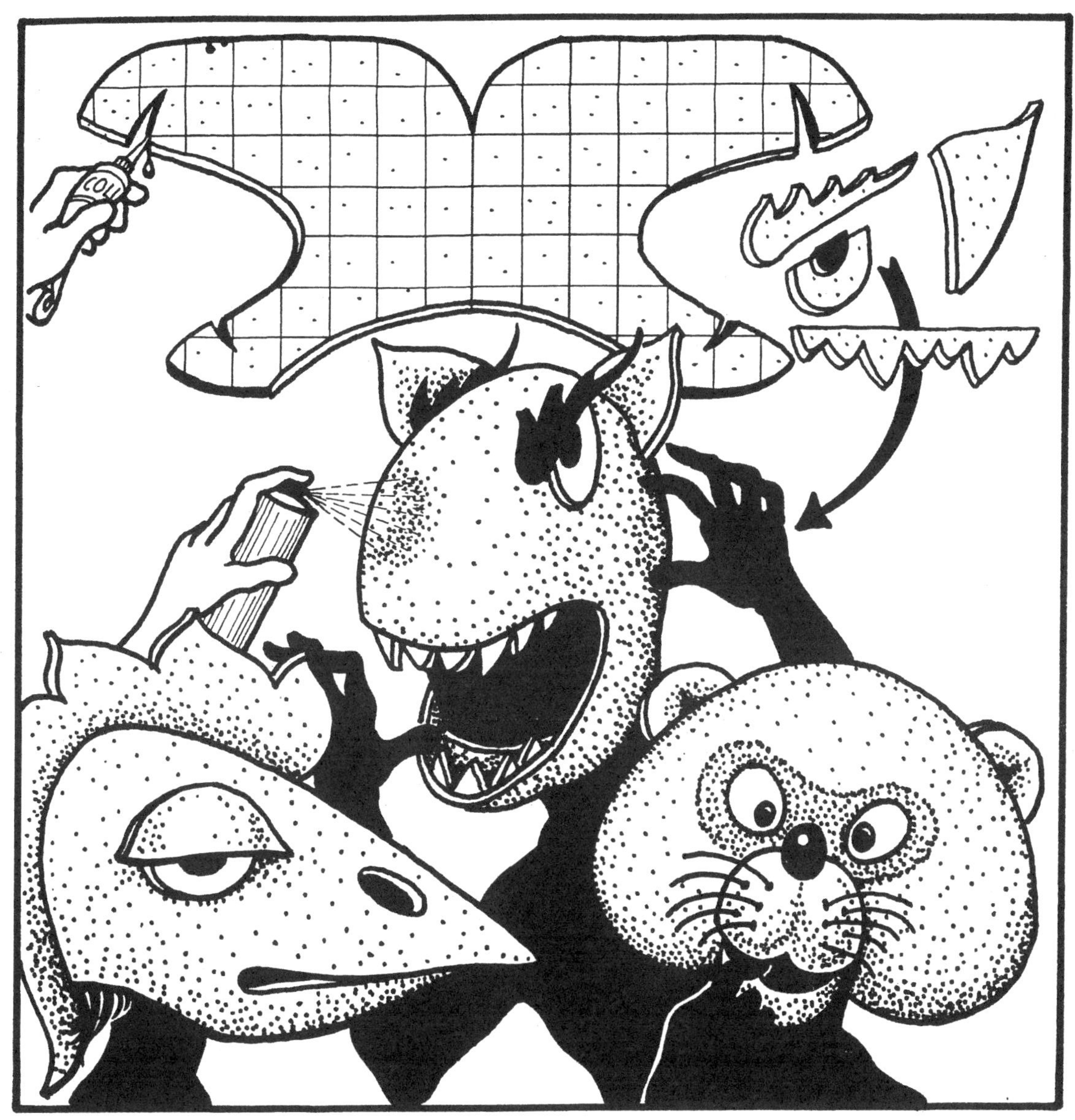

Masks The basic concept behind creating a foam-rubber mask is to connect two identical sides to obtain a sort of bag which, when worn, adapts to the form of the face. The masks can be of any shape but it is advisable to make them over-sized in order to allow the wearer's skin to breathe, since foam rubber is an insulating material. Even so, a closer fit can make movements of the jaw visible, for example when talking. This makes it possible to overcome the traditionally rigid facial features of papier-mâché masks

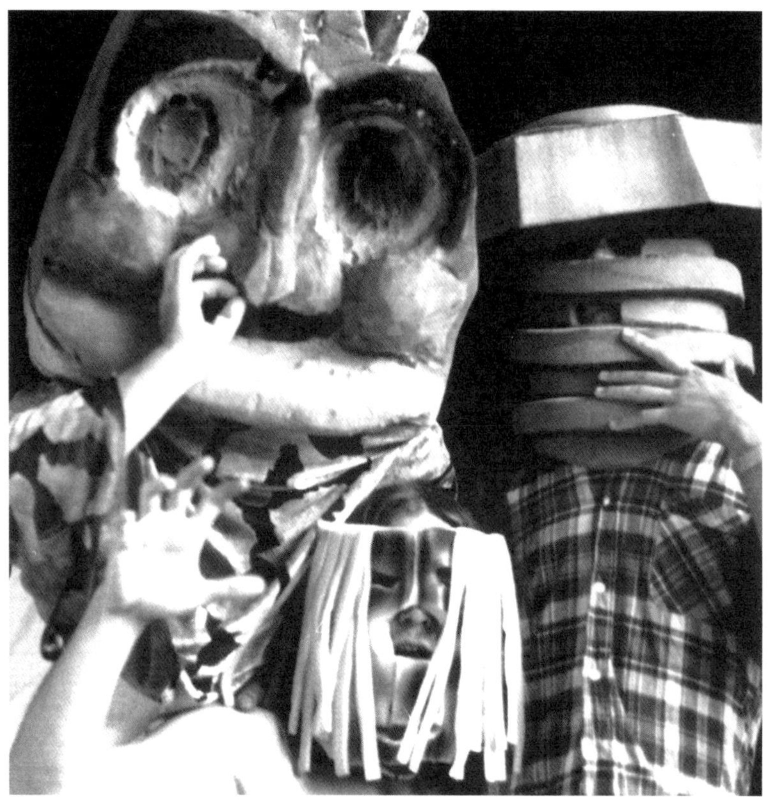

Spontaneaous Performance, Centri d'Incontro, Aurora district, Turin, 1980

DRAMATIZATION WITH FOAM RUBBER

One of the most important uses of foam rubber is in theater. From masks to puppets, through to Chinese serpent-dragons, almost all props for theater, street performances, and choreography can be made from foam rubber. The construction processes are quick and simple, leaving ample room for the imagination.

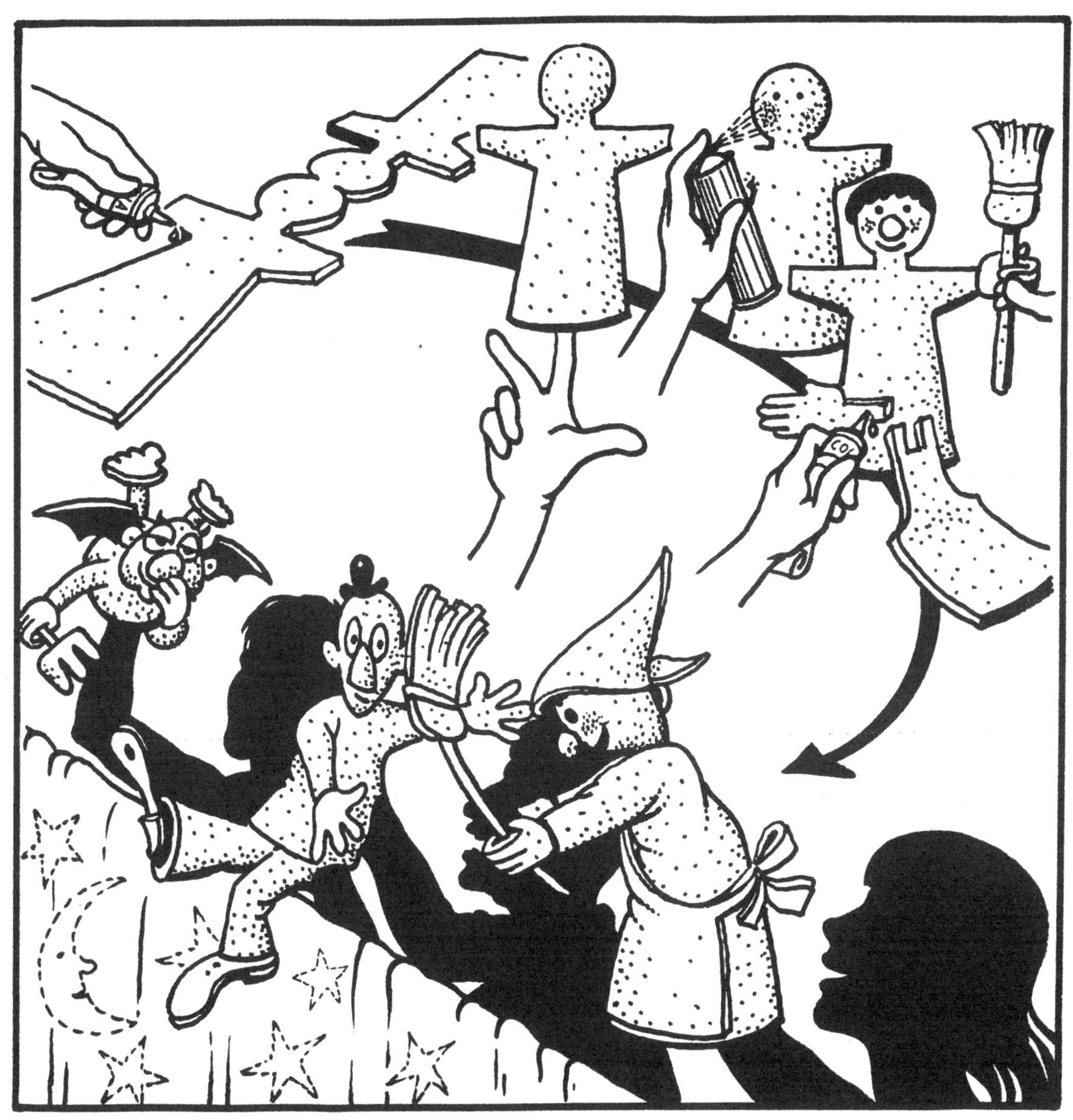

Glove puppets These can be made very easily from a sheet of foam rubber about 1 centimeter thick. The movements are, however, less subtle and vibrant than those of traditional fabric glove puppets, which means that the foam-rubber version will have a degree of expressive impact like that of an animated puppet.

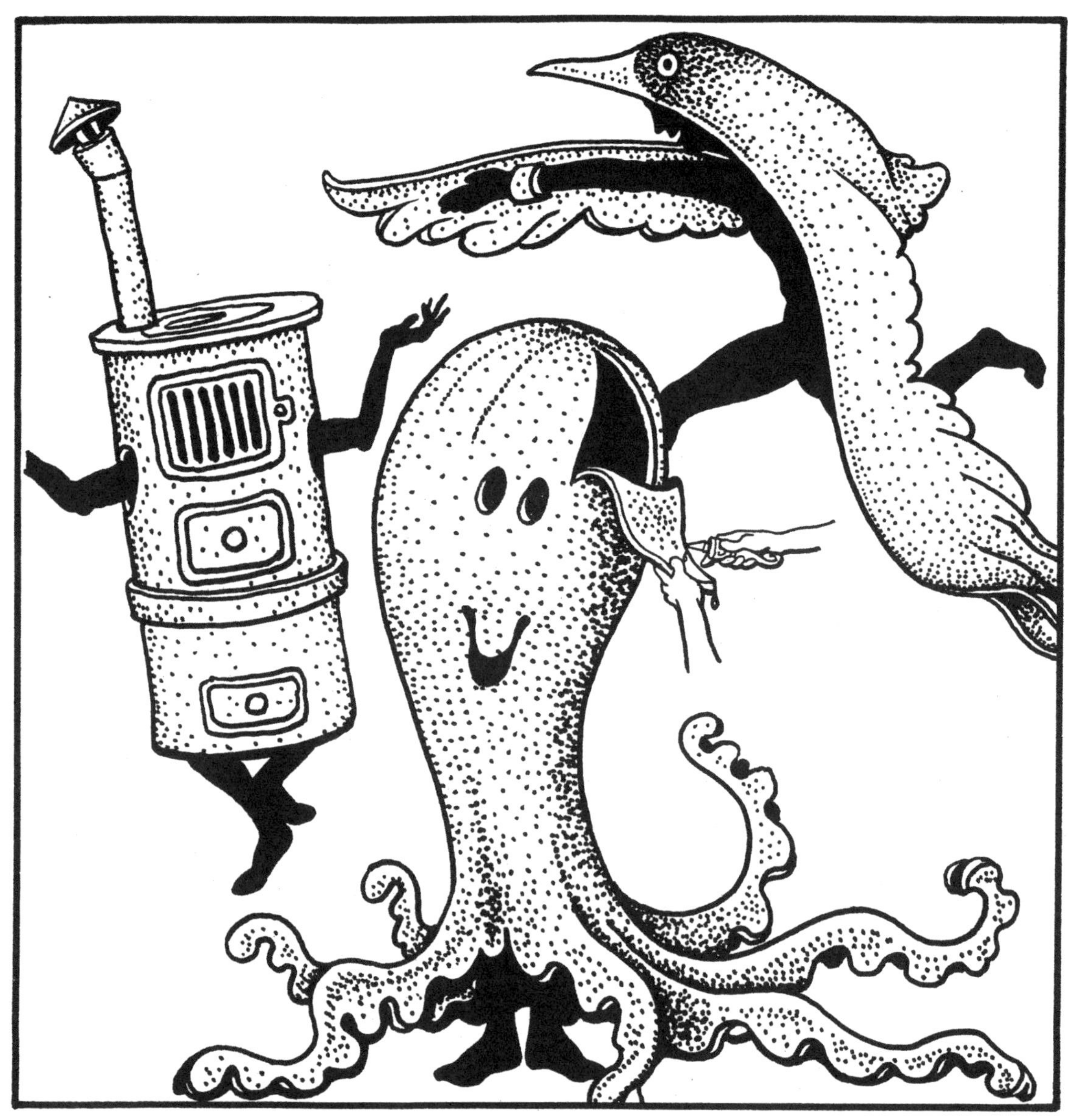

Costumes The ease with which foam rubber objects can adapt to the body, coupled with their lightness, means that it is possible to make costumes that reproduce a vast range of objects, from newspapers to stoves, to animals or locomotives. When reproducing living beings, the costumes can be made in a way that does not limit gestural expressiveness but rather enhances it in an ironic manner.

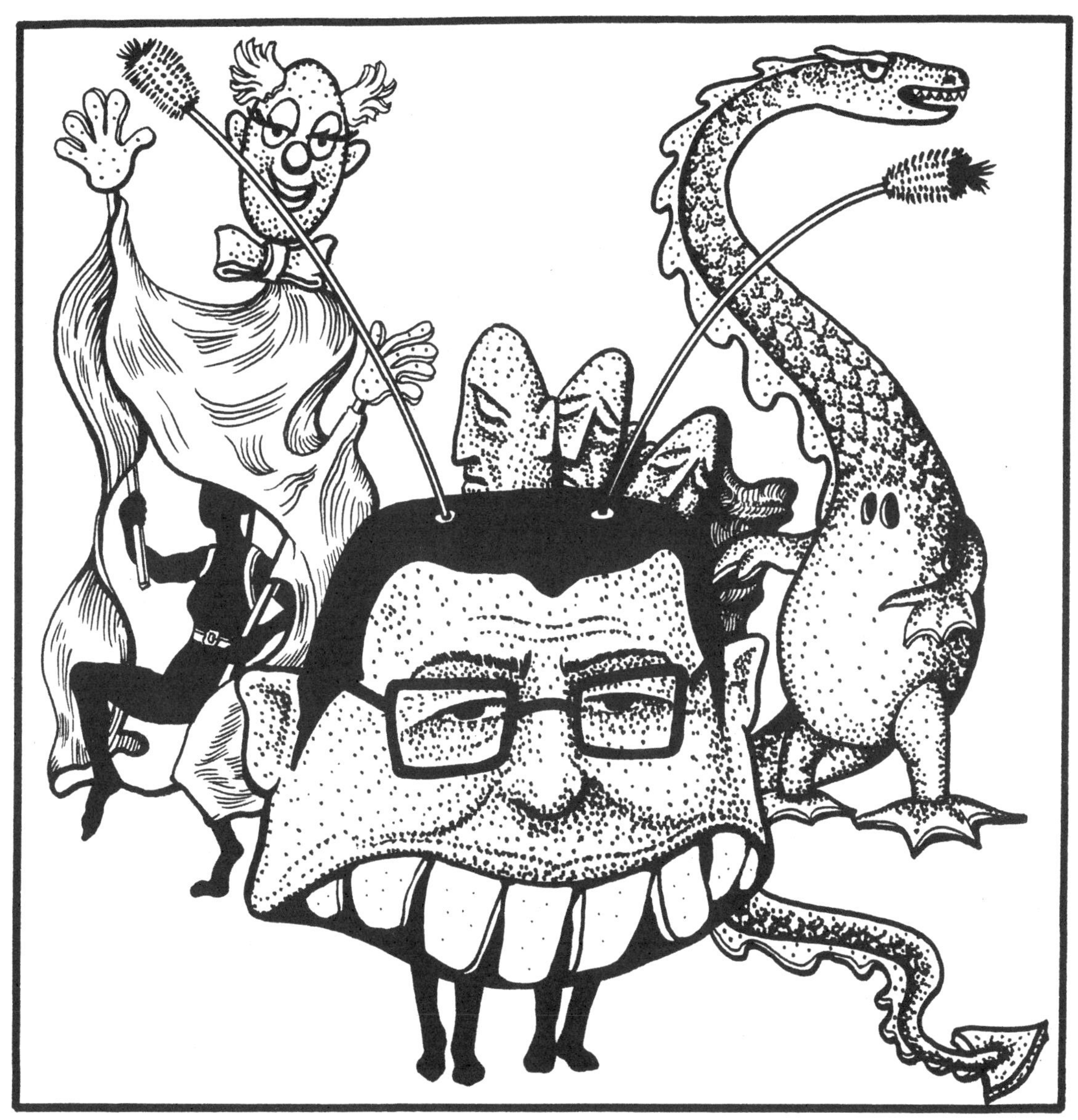

Giant figures When made of foam rubber, giant puppet costumes not only have their own intrinsic movement due to the characteristics of the material, which vibrates and sways at the slightest touch, they can also be brought to life by inserting elastic structures in them. These can be in the form of flexible, oscillating plastic tubes, or simple but effective mechanisms made of tie rods that make use of the flexibility of the material and its "rebound energy."

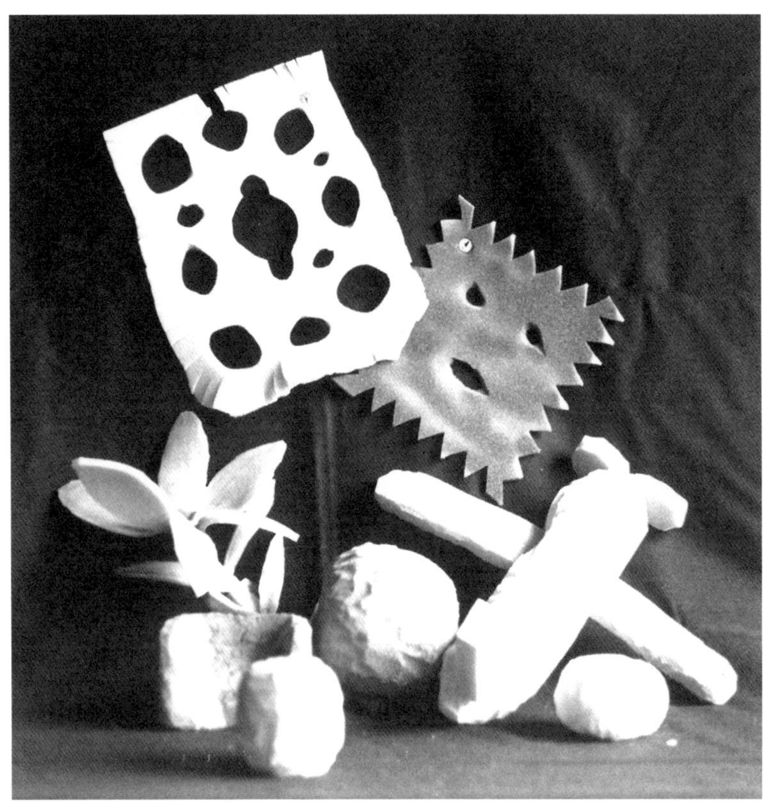

Art therapy workshop, Aurora district, Turin, 1977

SELF-EXPRESSION WITH FOAM RUBBER

Foam rubber can be used as a material for plastic expression to obtain special visual, tactile, and psychological effects, and the surface can be treated to achieve a wealth of effects such as roughness or a precious look. To obtain smooth or glossy surfaces, you need to use rubber latex varnish diluted in water and colored with the same pigments as those used for painting foam rubber.

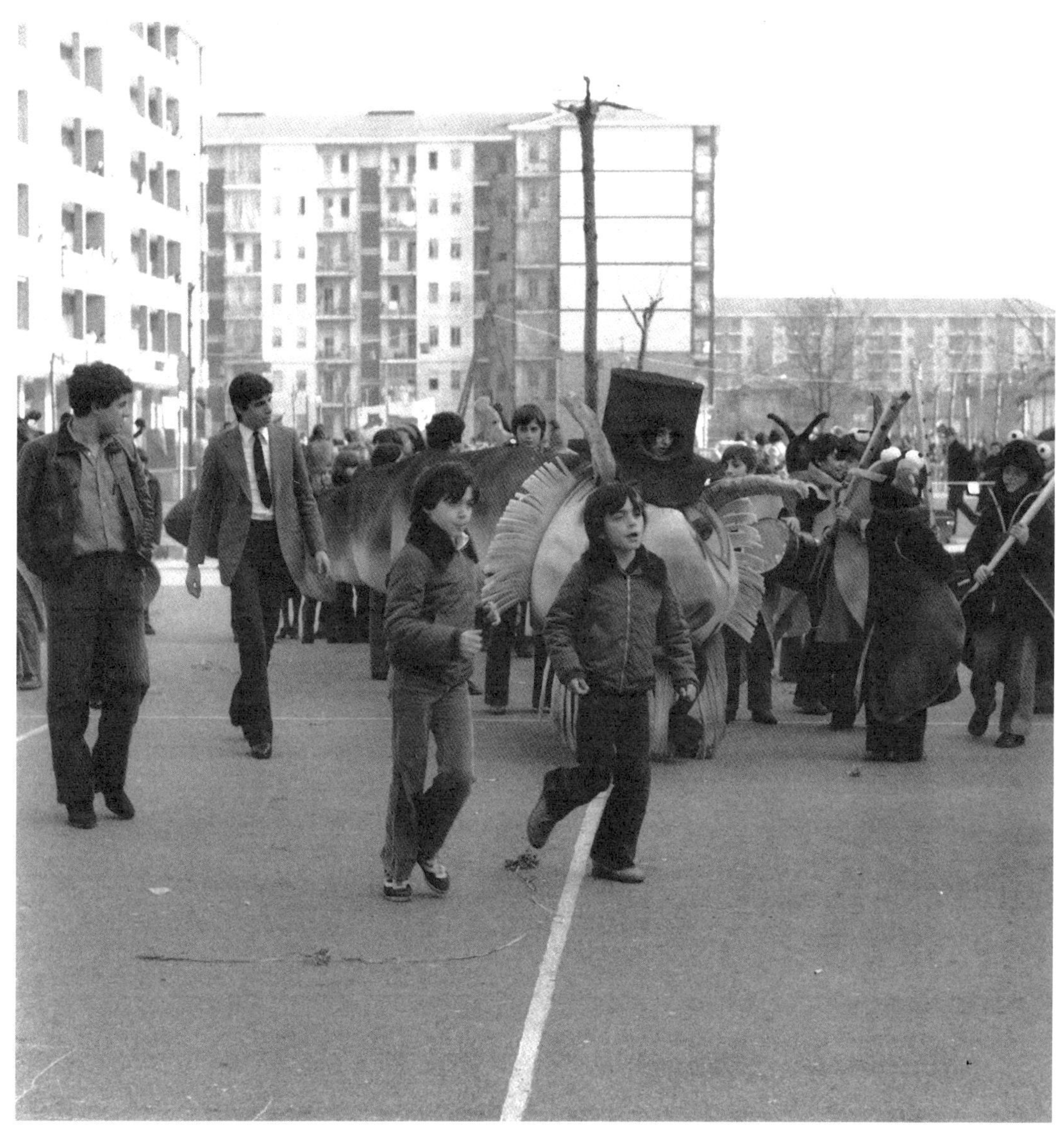

Serpents and group structures The basic serpent structure consists of a tube of foam rubber, about 4 centimeters thick, in which holes are made for the actors. This and other types of group structures offer far greater mobility than traditional systems due to the elasticity of the material used, and because they eliminate the need for rigid internal frames. They can also be used for movements that simulate violence—such as crashing into members of the audience or being attacked by them—thanks to the natural padding offered by the foam.

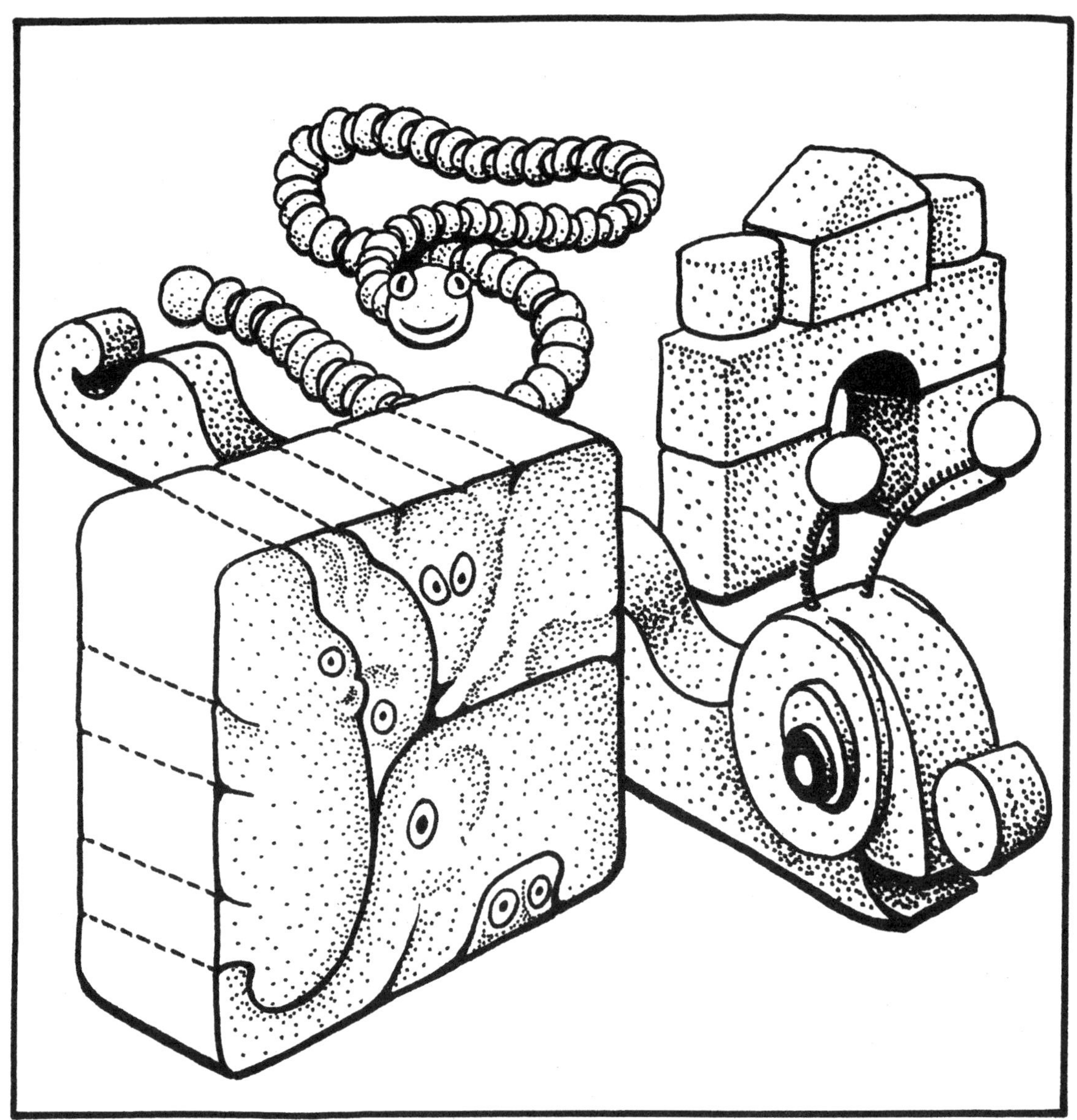

Simple, rapid cutting can be used to create bricks or other geometrical construction blocks, and a large block can be cut up to form a jigsaw puzzle of animals that can also be used on their own, or a giant caterpillar can be used by a whole group. Round sponges of different sizes can be stuck together to create the articulated body of a caterpillar, serpent, or other animal.

These oversized toys are ideal for some important educational experiences: the catharsis of aggression, socialization, and constructive research.

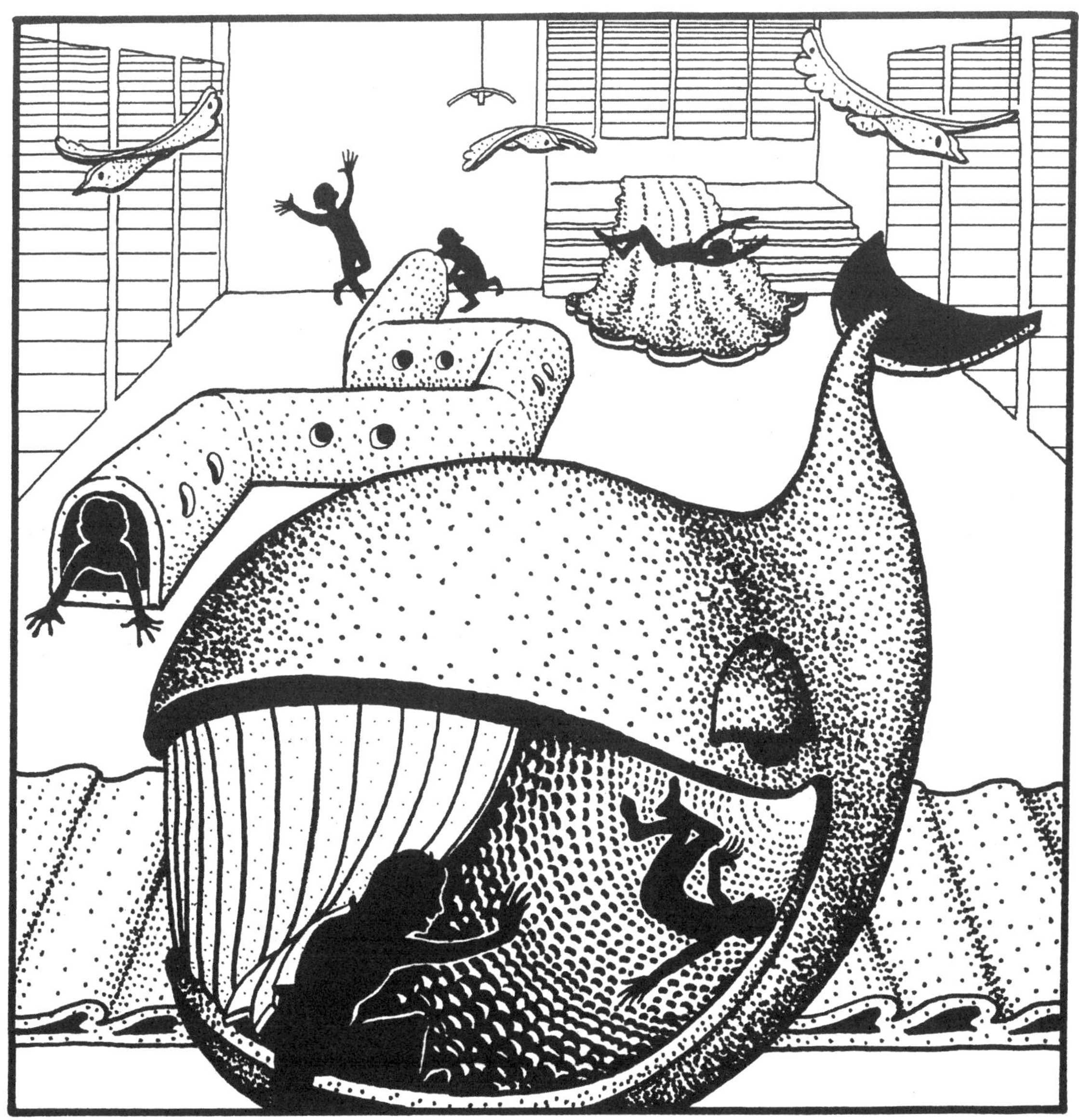

Environments The simplest way to create an environment using foam rubber is to modify the form of the floor, for example with a wavy carpet made with sheets about 5 centimeters thick. The very fact of walking on a soft surface is itself a stimulating experience for the effect it has on our sense of balance and on all the movements of our body. Another more complex possibility is to create closed spaces, such as a "whale's belly," which are both protective and sensorial. The interior forms an elastic delimitation of the space and an acoustic isolation that together forms an evident allusion to the maternal womb.

PROJECTS

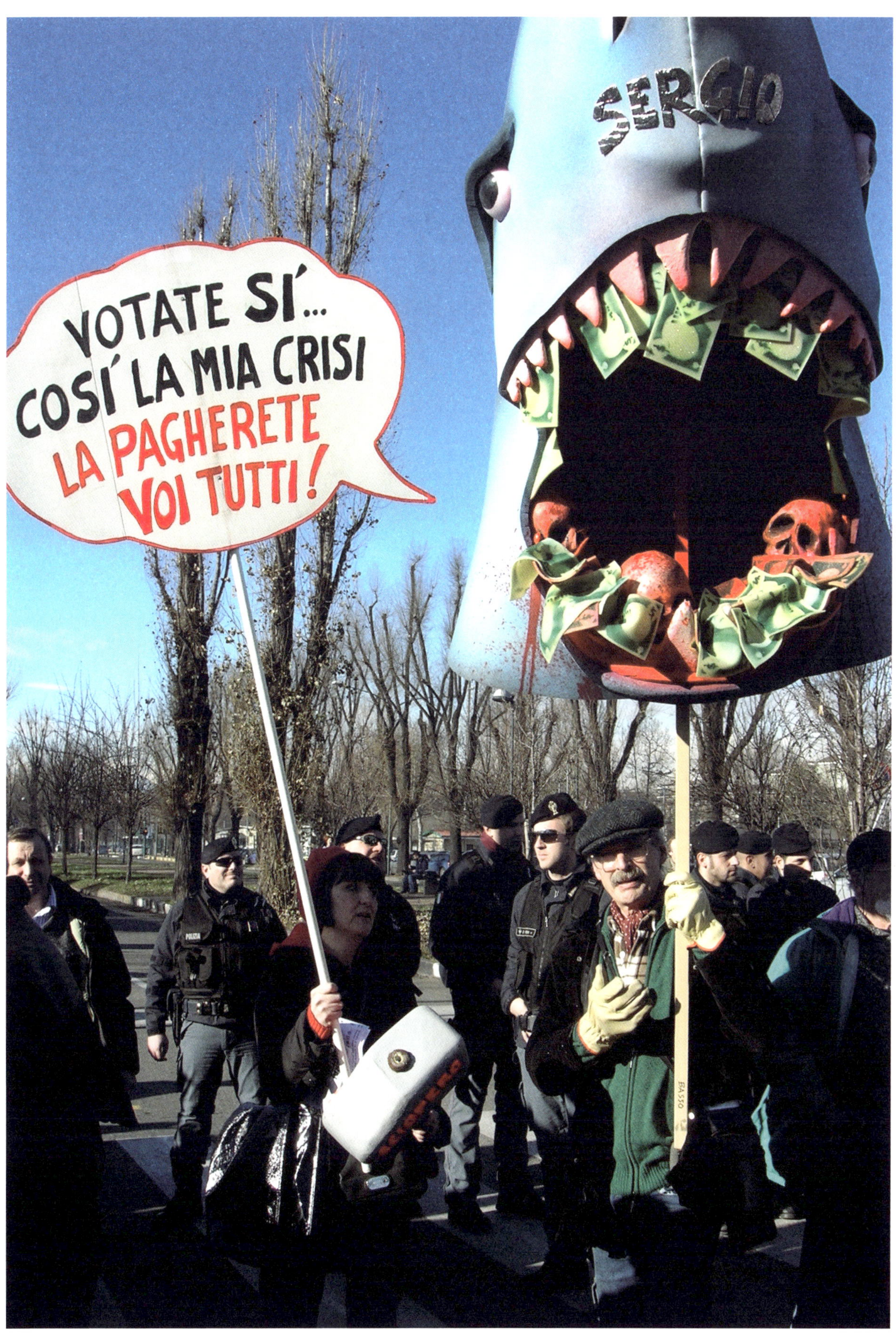
SERGIO
VOTATE SÍ...
COSÍ LA MIA CRISI
LA PAGHERETE
VOI TUTTI!

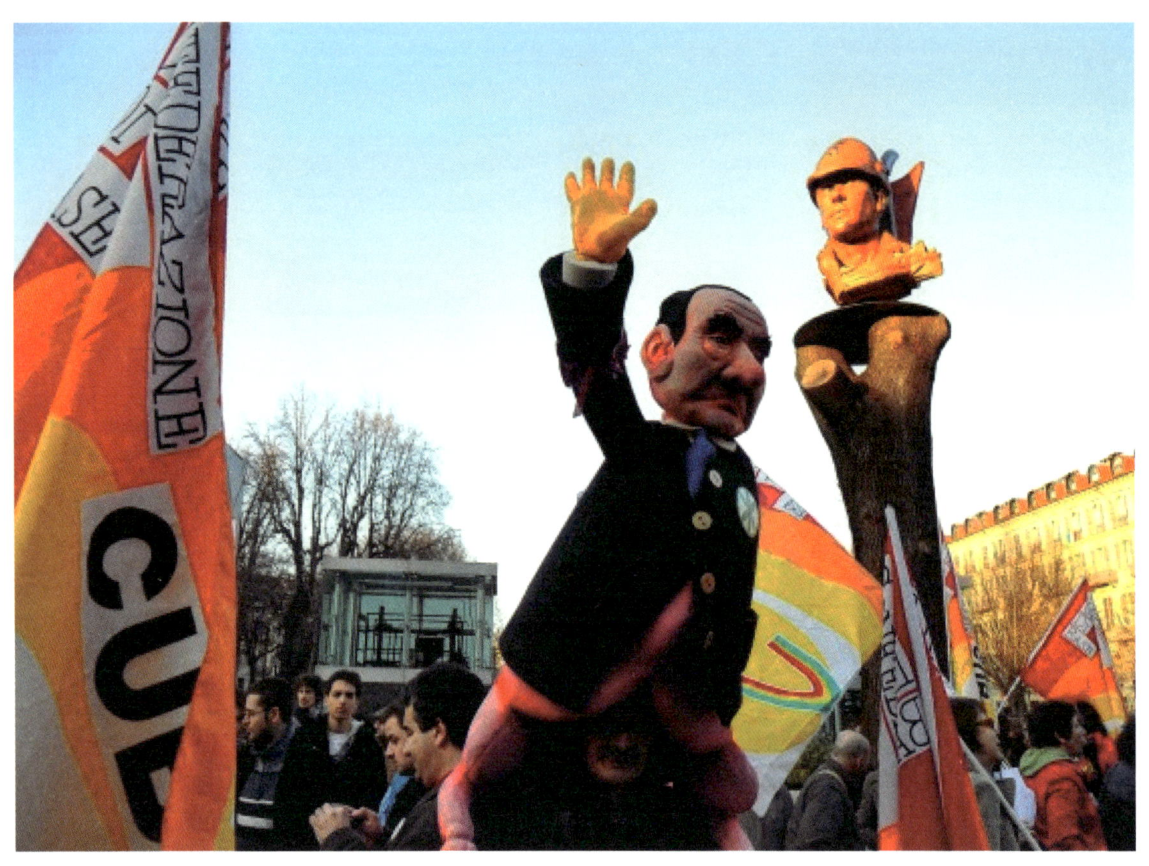

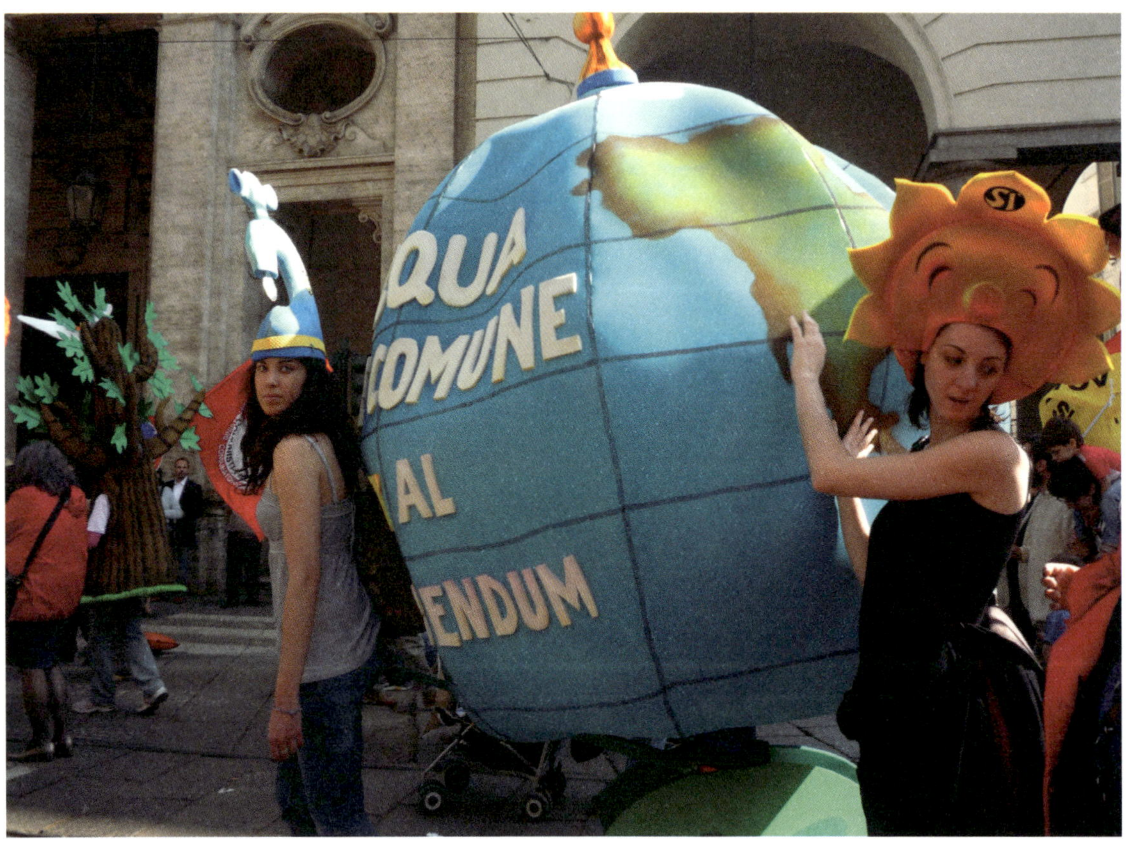
QUA
COMUNE
AL
ENDUM
SI

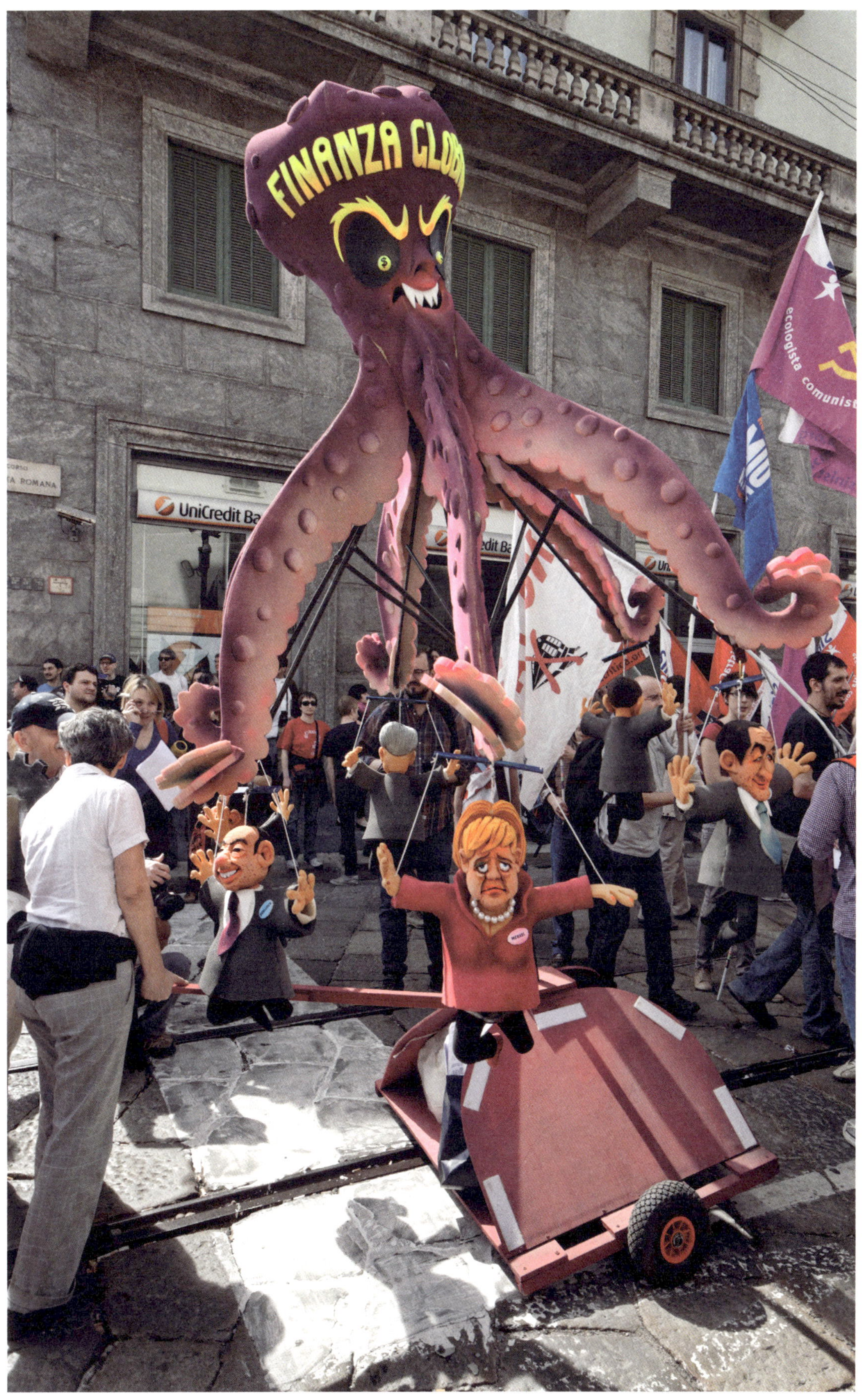
FINANZA
UniCredit
ecologista

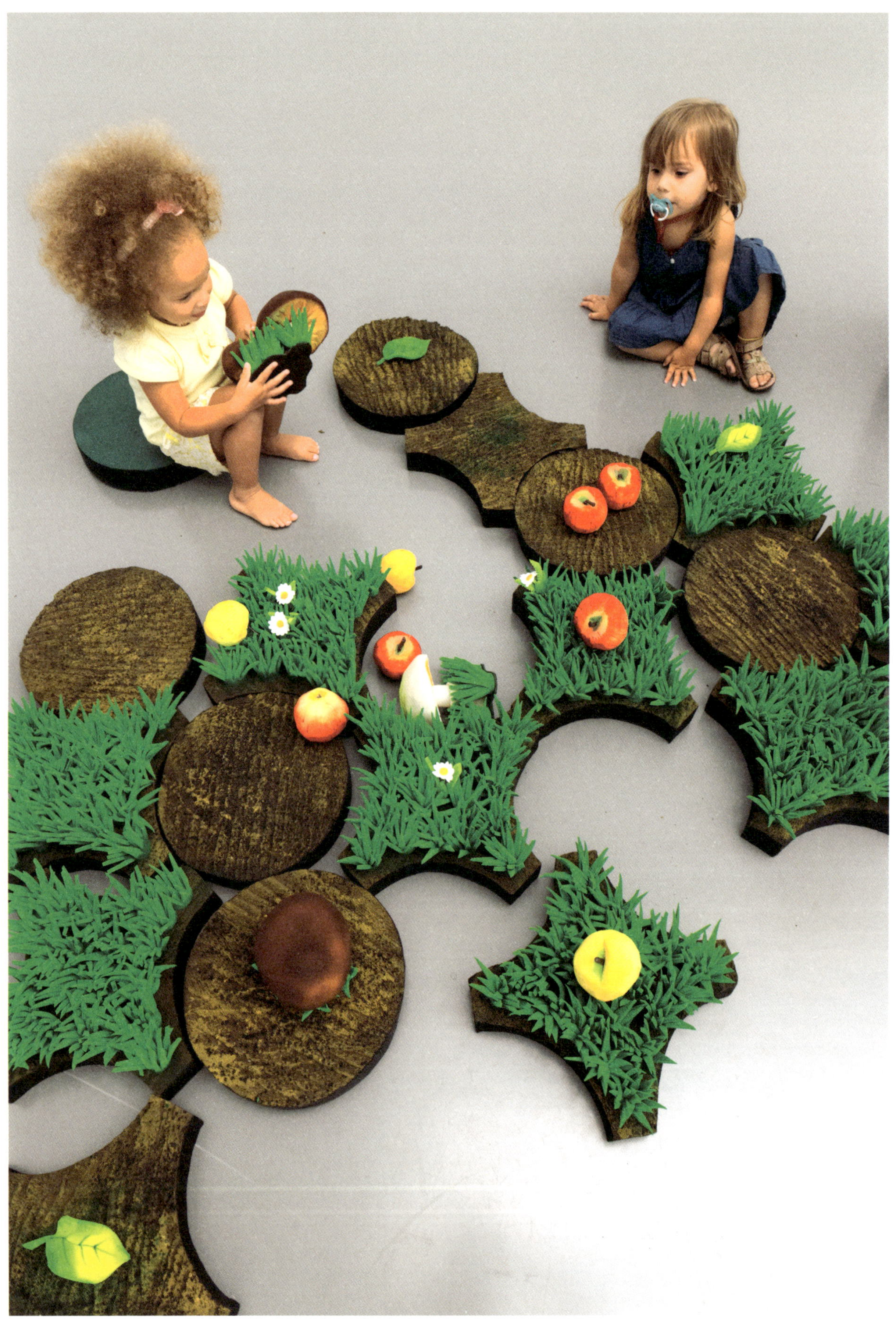

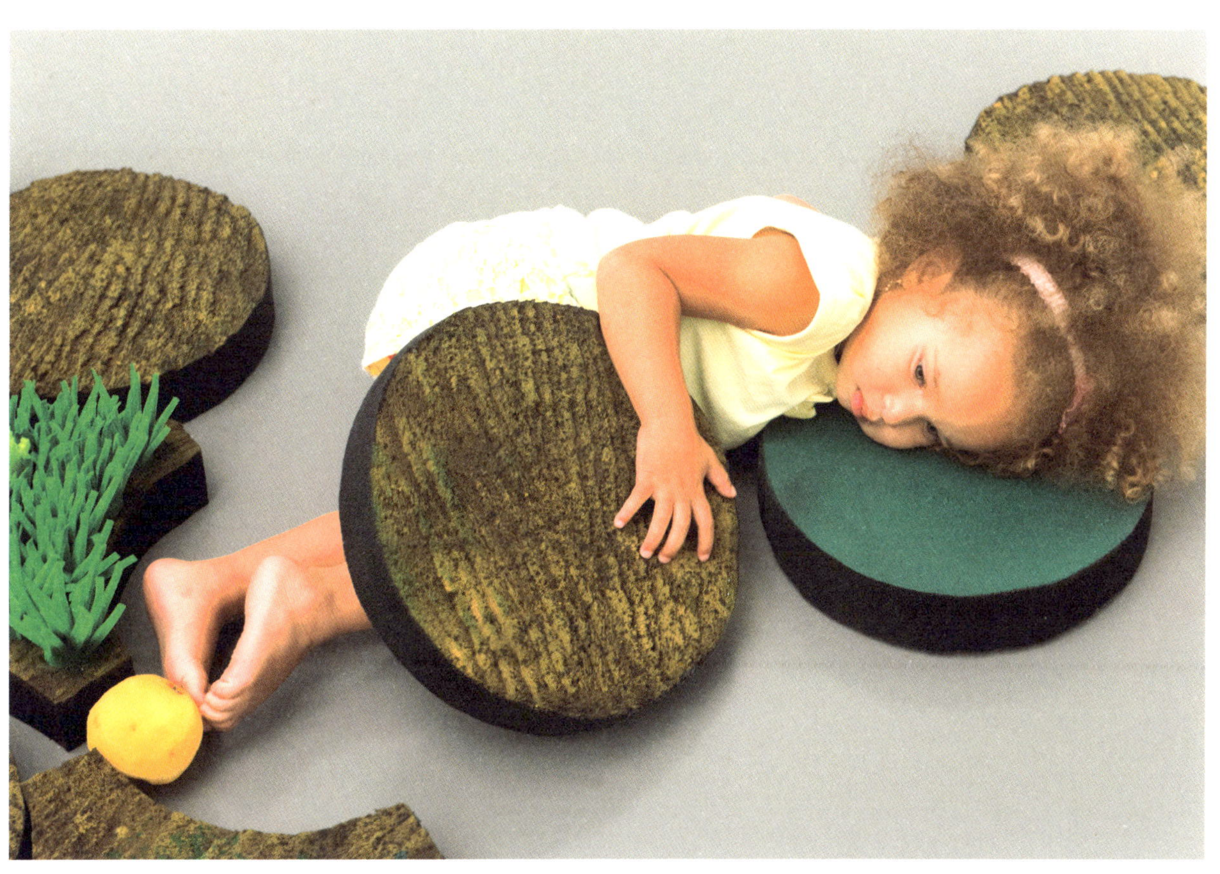

A CONVERSATION BETWEEN ANDREA BELLINI AND PIERO GILARDI ON "THE LITTLE MANUAL OF EXPRESSION WITH FOAM RUBBER"

October 2012

Andrea Bellini: Piero, when I saw the drafts for the manual on foam rubber in your archive, I immediately felt it would be important to publish it. What struck me was this need of yours to offer the public a technique, a system of knowledge you've acquired through your artistic and political actions. Did this little manual come from a desire to offer a new instrument of expression to the young, politically engaged generations?

Piero Gilardi: I think the main purpose of the manual is to provide a means of expression to the younger generations, who are entering a society that is alienating in terms of both subjectivity and human relations. Despite the colonization of our individual consciousness by the mass media, social studies have shown that there's still huge potential for creativity, which is constantly in search of new expressive openings. According to the French philosopher Bernard Stiegler, the consumer system is based on a diversion of the individual's libido toward the rituals of shopping, and all those impulses that escape this mechanism tend quite simply to produce artistic expression.[1] Even so, the issue of techné, fully liberating creativity through mastery of a symbolic language, still remains.

Today's telecommunication networks and social networks certainly offer common "global" spaces for symbolic expression and interaction, but the concept contained in *The Little Manual of Expression with Foam Rubber* has the added value of corporal expression. Foam-rubber puppets, costumes, and masks adhere to the body like gloves and thus constitute a system of signs capable of catalyzing total emotional involvement in a fully relational performative action. This is what we see taking place in the political expressions of today's movements, which range from the occupation of symbolic places to human chains and flash mobs.

You were the first to use foam rubber in the 1960s. Could you tell me how this idea came about? And your famous nature-carpets?

I had the urge to create my nature-carpets in 1967, while I was walking along the bed of one of the five rivers of Turin, my home town. It was polluted by a revolting amount of urban and industrial refuse and it was there that I felt the desire to recreate a pristine natural setting, using a material that is soft and inviting for our bodies, in the form of a normal household carpet. As Ettore Sottsass[2] wrote, it was a symbolic gesture to exorcise the killing and death of nature but also, as Nicolas Bourriaud would say, of a "utopia of proximity,"[3] for the implicit relational nature given by a convivial object such as a household carpet.

In the 1970s you started using foam rubber for your Agitprop (agitation propaganda) activities of social and political commitment. Was this a group work? How did the masks and objects for use during public protests and marches come about, and how do they come about today?

The 1970s brought a conceptual leap in the use of foam rubber, which was transformed from a technique used to reinvent the habitat to an instrument used to recreate the habitus. This shift was made possible by the affinity between the "biomorphic" aspect of foam rubber (which is a simulation of sea sponges) and our body. At the time, I was an activist in the La Comune di Torino political-artistic

---

[1] Introduction to the symposium "Art et Politique. Rencontres d'Arles," July 6, 2005.

[2] "Memorie di panna montata," *Domus*, 445, Milano, 1966.

[3] *L'esthétique relationnelle,* Les Presses du réel, Dijon, 1996.

collective, which made banners, posters, and photographic exhibitions for the political struggle. We had the idea of making large masks of our political opponents and going to jeer at them during their rallies and public appearances. Our projects later became increasingly complex, leading to participatory political drama performances in the city squares, which we also put on for the First of May processions. These have continued over the years, right up to the present day.

The concepts and productions have always been the result of collective work and, by organizing preparatory workshops on foam-rubber processing techniques, the creative subjects have multiplied to the point where you can now find masks and costumes made with this material in almost all political protests in the streets.

Since the 1980s, Pietro Perotti—an authentic artist-worker who currently makes costumes and theater sets for Stefano Benni and Altan—has played a part in the proliferation of the theatrical use of foam rubber.

Your extraordinary familiarity with this material has made you a landmark figure in the art world. For example, you've been a consultant to artists like Claes Oldenburg, John Chamberlain, Gaetano Pesce, and other young artists. Which of these collaboration and "consultancy" experiences have been most significant and interesting for you?
I think that for me the most significant experience of working with other artists was with Oldenburg in 1985. He was preparing a spectacular public performance, his famous *The Course of the Knife* for the Venice Biennale, and he asked me to make a huge ball with household objects—chairs, tables, a step ladder—tied onto it, which would then be crushed as it rolled. I was very pleased to work with him, not just because I felt in tune with the spirit of his participatory performance, but also because I wanted to express my gratitude to him for having inspired me in the 1960s with his "soft" poetic vision, with the aesthetic adoption of foam rubber as a raw material of expression.

Many museum curators and collectors are afraid of the fragility of this material and of its degradability. Is there something you'd like to say about the problem of preserving these objects?
Like almost all polymers, foam rubber, or rather expanded polyurethane, has a limited chemical life, estimated at around 25 years. I found that this aspect was consistent with the transitory nature of the experience I wanted to offer through interaction with my nature-carpets, which could be worn out by use as well as being biodegradable.

Even so, first my experience in the world of design, and then the realization that collectors and museums needed guarantees about the permanency of my works, led me—with the help of a chemical engineer—to seek a technical solution that could protect foam rubber from the agent that degrades it, which is the ultraviolet component of daylight. So ever since the 1970s—and today in the restoration of historic works from the previous decade—my foam-rubber works have been protected by an insulating blend of rubber latex and another ten chemical elements, including zinc oxide, which is universally used as a protective barrier against ultraviolet rays.

Let's end with a sort of game. If there were only enough foam rubber left in the world to write a single word, what word would you write, after your five decades of artistic and political activity?
Well, to play along with the game, this is the phrase I'd cut out: "NOTHING IS CREATED. EVERYTHING CHANGES."